श्रीः

Enjoyable Sanskrit Grammar

Volume **1**

Basic Structure of the Language

Workbook

Name: _____

Electronic version of this book is available at:
Arsha Avinash Foundation
www.arshaavinash.in

Printed version of this book is available at:
Arsha Vidya Gurukulam, Coimbatore, TN, India
www.arshavidya.in
Swami Dayananda Ashram, Rishikesh, UK, India
www.dayananda.org
Arsha Vidya Gurukulam, Saylorsburg, PA, USA
www.arshavidya.org
CreateSpace
www.createspace.com (Search by "medha michika")
Amazon of your country
www.amazon.com etc. (Search by "medha michika")

Tutorial videos to accompany this series of books will soon be available
online. Search YouTube under "Medha Sanskrit".

How to use this book

1. Write

    in full colour, with all your creativity.

2. Memorize

    finding ways to utilize your mindasyou want.

3. Recite

    what you have memorized to your teacher.

4. Share

    with generosity

Table of Contents

Prayer

1.

2.

3.

4.

5.

Topic I

Letters/Sounds

Diphthongs: _____

Special letters/sounds which come after vowel: ं ṃ _____,   ः ḥ _____

What is the name for short vowel in Sanskrit? _____

What is the name for long vowel in Sanskrit? _____

What are गुण [guṇa] letters? _____

What are वृद्धि [vṛddhi] letters? _____

Vowels:

There are 9 vowels in Sanskrit:

- 5 simple vowels –   short form: _____

                          (long form: _____

- 4 diphthongs -   long   _____

Consonants:

There are 33 consonants in Sanskrit.

- 25 consonants = 5 categories x 5 classes

  _____

  _____

  _____

  _____

  _____

- 4 Semivowels   _____

- 4 Sibilants   _____

Topic II

Structure of the Sanskrit Language

Building Blocks of the Sanskrit Language

☐ _____ (_____ [_____]) is a unit of expression to communicate an idea.

☐ A _____ consists of _____ (_____ [_____]) or _____ (_____ [_____]).

_____ [_____] (sentence)

_____ [__] (word)   _____ [__] (word)   _____ [__] (word)

_____ [_____] (words)

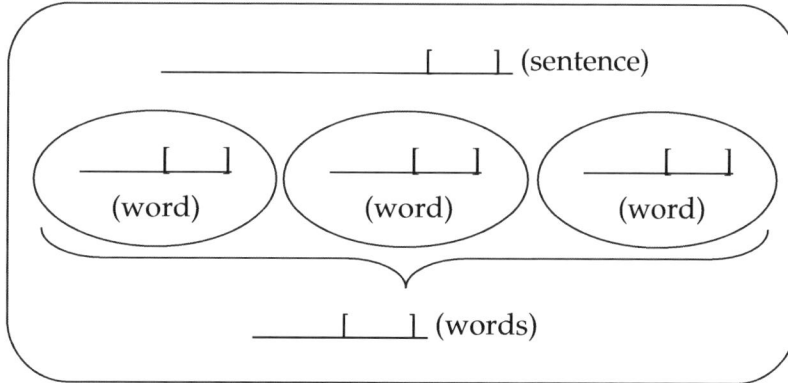

☐ In the Sanskrit language, there are only two types of words:

  1. Verb _____ [_____]

  2. Noun _____ [_____]

☐ Every word in Sanskrit is comprised of two basic constituents:

_____(_____[____]) + _____(_____[____])

(_____[__]) = (_____[__]) + (_____[__])
(word)   (original entity)   (suffix)

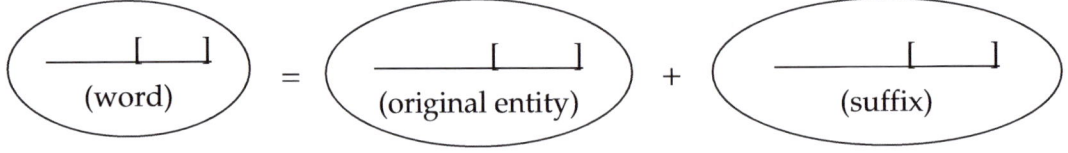

1. Verb (तिङन्तं पदम् [tiṅantaṃ padam]) :

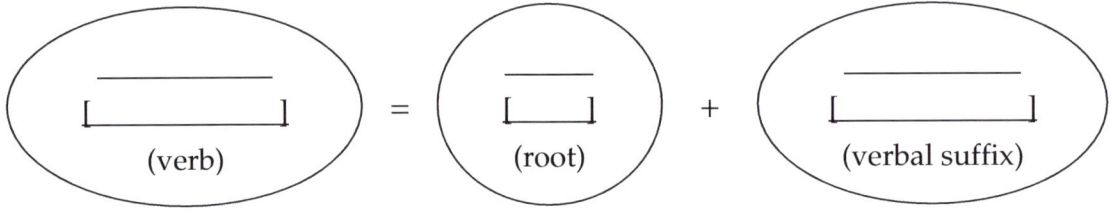

(_____[_____]) = ([___]) + ([_____])
(verb)   (root)   (verbal suffix)

2. Noun (सुबन्तं पदम् [subantaṃ padam]):

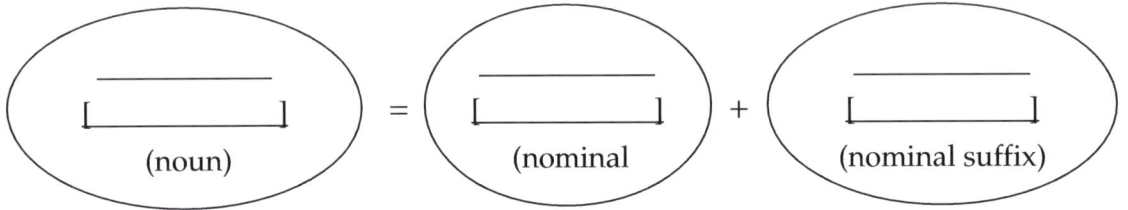

([_____]) = ([_____]) + ([_____])
(noun)   (nominal   (nominal suffix)

☐ There are two types of suffix (प्रत्ययः [pratyayaḥ]) to make a word (पदम् [padam]).

1. Verbal suffix (_____[_____])

2. Nominal suffix (_____[_____])

☐ In every sentence there is one verb (_____[_____]), written or implied.

Topic III

Factors of action

कारकम्

☐ What is कारक?

☐ कारकs are 6 in number.

1. _____   [_____]   (_____)

2. _____   [_____]   (_____)

3. _____   [_____]   (_____)

4. _____   [_____]   (_____)

5. _____   [_____]   (_____)

6. _____   [_____]   (_____)

Original forms of तिङ्-प्रत्ययs

Original forms of सुप्-प्रत्ययs

Topic IV

The Concept of

Verbs (तिङन्तम् [tiṅantam])

2. Constituents of verb (तिङन्तम् [tiṅantam])

_____ (_____ [_____])

= _____ (_____ [_____]) + _____ (_____ [_____])

3. Classifications of धातु [dhātu] (Verbal root)

    i. _____ groups of conjugations (_____ to _____)

    ii. _____ types (_____, _____, and _____)

4. Ten लकार [lakāra]s

1. _____ [____]

2. _____ [____]

3. _____ [____]

4. _____ [____]

5. _____ [____]

6. _____ [____]

7. _____ [____]

8. _____ [____]

9. _____ [____]

10. _____ [____]

लकार [lakāra] represents two things.

i. Voice (प्रयोगः [prayogah])

There are three voices for verb. They are:

a) _____ (_____ [_____])

b) _____ (_____ [_____])

c) _____ (_____ [_____])

ii. Tense and mood

1. _____ can be used in _____ .

2. _____ can be used in _____ .

3. _____ can be used in _____ .

4. _____ can be used in _____ .

5. _____ can be used in _____ .

6. _____ can be used in _____ .

7. _____ can be used in _____ .

8. _____ can be used in _____ .

9. _____ can be used in _____ .

10. _____ can be used in _____ .

5. Verbal suffix (तिङ्-प्रत्ययः [tiṅ-pratyayaḥ])

तिङ्-प्रत्यय s further denote two more things.

    i. Person (_____ [_____])

    ii. Number (_____ [_____])

i. Person (पुरुषः [puruṣaḥ])

There are three persons, as described in the chart below.

Person	In Sanskrit	Who?	Examples

ii. Number (वचनम् [vacanam])

There are three numbers, as described in the matrix with persons in the chart below.

Number / Person	Singular	Dual	Plural

Two पद [pada]s

There are eighteen तिङ्-प्रत्ययs. As seen in the chart below, they are divided into two sets of nine. They are:

- _____ [   ]

- _____ [   ]

Topic V

Conjugation in लट् (present tense)

1. लट् (Present Tense) in कर्तरि प्रयोगः (Active Voice)

with परस्मैपदी धातुः (Parasmaipadī dhātuḥ)

परस्मैपद of तिङ्-प्रत्ययs modified for लट् (present tense)

Final forms

- धातुः (root):   भू (_____) _____
- लकारः (tense/mood):   _____
- प्रयोगः (voice):   _____
- अङ्गम् (stem):   _____

Topic V – Conjugation in लट् (Present tense)

- **धातुः (root):** कृष् (____) _____
- **लकारः (tense/mood):** _____
- **प्रयोगः (voice):** _____
- **अङ्गम् (stem):** _____

- **धातुः (root):** गम् (____) _____
- **लकारः (tense/mood):** _____
- **प्रयोगः (voice):** _____
- **अङ्गम् (stem):** _____

Topic V – Conjugation in लट् (Present tense)

- _____ : चर् (___)_____
- _____ : _____
- _____ : _____
- _____ : _____

- _____ : जीव् (___)_____
- _____ : _____
- _____ : _____
- _____ : _____

Topic V – Conjugation in लट् (Present tense)

- _____ : दृश् (___) _____
- _____ : _____
- _____ : _____
- _____ : _____

- _____ : नम् (___) _____
- _____ : _____
- _____ : _____
- _____ : _____

Topic V – Conjugation in लट् (Present tense)

- _____ :   नी (_____) _____
- _____ :   _____
- _____ :   _____
- _____ :   _____

- _____ :   पठ् (_____) _____
- _____ :   _____
- _____ :   _____
- _____ :   _____

- _____ : पत् (_____) _____

- _____ : _____

- _____ : _____

- _____ : _____

- _____ : बुध् (_____) _____

- _____ : _____

- _____ : _____

- _____ : _____

Topic V – Conjugation in लट् (Present tense)

- _____ : वस् (___) _____
- _____ : _____
- _____ : _____
- _____ : _____

- _____ : स्था (___) _____
- _____ : _____
- _____ : _____
- _____ : _____

Topic V – Conjugation in लट् (Present tense)

- _____ : सृ (____) _____
- _____ : _____
- _____ : _____
- _____ : _____

- _____ : अस् (____) _____
- _____ : _____
- _____ : _____
- _____ : _____

Topic V – Conjugation in लट् (Present tense)

- _____ : नश् (____) _____

- _____ : _____

- _____ : _____

- _____ : _____

- _____ : तुष् (____) _____

- _____ : _____

- _____ : _____

- _____ : _____

Topic V – Conjugation in लट् (Present tense)

- _____ : नृत् (___) _____

- _____ : _____

- _____ : _____

- _____ : _____

- _____ : पुष् (___) _____

- _____ : _____

- _____ : _____

- _____ : _____

Topic V – Conjugation in लट् (Present tense)

- _____ : मुह् (____) _____
- _____ : _____
- _____ : _____
- _____ : _____

- _____ : शुष् (____) _____
- _____ : _____
- _____ : _____
- _____ : _____

- _____ : इष् (____) _____
- _____ : _____
- _____ : _____
- _____ : _____

- _____ : दिश् (____) _____
- _____ : _____
- _____ : _____
- _____ : _____

Topic V – Conjugation in लट् (Present tense)

- _____ : प्रच्छ् (   ) _____
- _____ : _____
- _____ : _____
- _____ : _____

- _____ : मुच् (   ) _____
- _____ : _____
- _____ : _____
- _____ : _____

Topic V – Conjugation in लट् (Present tense)

- _____ : विद् (____) _____
- _____ : _____
- _____ : _____
- _____ : _____

- _____ : स्पृश (____) _____
- _____ : _____
- _____ : _____
- _____ : _____

Topic V – Conjugation in लट् (Present tense)

- _____ :   लिख (   ) _____
- _____ :   _____
- _____ :   _____
- _____ :   _____

- _____ :   विश (   ) _____
- _____ :   _____
- _____ :   _____
- _____ :   _____

Topic V – Conjugation in लट् (Present tense)

- _____ : सृज (____) _____
- _____ : _____
- _____ : _____
- _____ : _____

- _____ : अस् (____) _____
- _____ : _____
- _____ : _____
- _____ : _____

Topic V – Conjugation in लट् (Present tense)

- _____ : कृ (____) _____
- _____ : _____
- _____ : _____
- _____ : _____

- _____ : ज्ञा (____) _____
- _____ : _____
- _____ : _____
- _____ : _____

- _____ :   आप (___) _____

- _____ :   _____

- _____ :   _____

- _____ :   _____

- _____ :   विद् (___) _____

- _____ :   _____

- _____ :   _____

- _____ :   _____

2. Consulting धातुकोशः [dhātukośaḥ]

Manners of modification of simple vowels

Modification / Original	इ	उ	ऋ

3. उपसर्गाः [upasargāḥ] (Verbal prefixes)

1. ___[___]   2. ___[___]   3. ___[___]   4. ___[___]   5. ___[___]

6. ___[___]   7. ___[___]   8. ___[___]   9. ___[___]   10. ___[___]

11. ___[___]   12. ___[___]   13. ___[___]   14. ___[___]   15. ___[___]

16. ___[___]   17. ___[___]   18. ___[___]   19. ___[___]   20. ___[___]

21. ___[___]   22. ___[___]

4. लट् (Present Tense) in कर्तरि प्रयोगः (Active Voice)

with आत्मनेपदी धातुः (Ātmanepadī root)

आत्मनेपद of तिङ्-प्रत्ययs modified for लट् (present tense)

- _____ : ईक्ष् (____) _____
- _____ : _____
- _____ : _____
- _____ : _____

- _____ : काश् (___) _____

- _____ : _____

- _____ : _____

- _____ : _____

- _____ : बाध् (___) _____

- _____ : _____

- _____ : _____

- _____ : _____

Topic V – Conjugation in लट् (Present tense)

- _____ : भाष (____)_____

- _____ : _____

- _____ : _____

- _____ : _____

- _____ : मुद् (____)_____

- _____ : _____

- _____ : _____

- _____ : _____

Topic V – Conjugation in लट् (Present tense)

- _____ : यत् (____) _____
- _____ : _____
- _____ : _____
- _____ : _____

- _____ : रम् (____) _____
- _____ : _____
- _____ : _____
- _____ : _____

Topic V – Conjugation in लट् (Present tense)

- _____ : लभ् (____) _____

- _____ : _____

- _____ : _____

- _____ : _____

- _____ : वृत् (____) _____

- _____ : _____

- _____ : _____

- _____ : _____

Topic V – Conjugation in लट् (Present tense)

- _____ : शङ्क् ( ) _____
- _____ : _____
- _____ : _____
- _____ : _____

- _____ : शुभ् ( ) _____
- _____ : _____
- _____ : _____
- _____ : _____

Topic V – Conjugation in लट् (Present tense)

- _____ : सह् (____) _____
- _____ : _____
- _____ : _____
- _____ : _____

- _____ : सेव् (____) _____
- _____ : _____
- _____ : _____
- _____ : _____

Topic V – Conjugation in लट् (Present tense)

- _____ : जन् (____) _____
- _____ : _____
- _____ : _____
- _____ : _____

- _____ : पद् (____) _____
- _____ : _____
- _____ : _____
- _____ : _____

Topic V – Conjugation in लट् (Present tense)

- _____ : बुध(___) _____
- _____ : _____
- _____ : _____
- _____ : _____

- _____ : मन् (___) _____
- _____ : _____
- _____ : _____
- _____ : _____

- _____ : युध् (____) _____

- _____ : _____

- _____ : _____

- _____ : _____

- _____ : विद् (____) _____

- _____ : _____

- _____ : _____

- _____ : _____

- _____ : सृज् (___) _____

- _____ : _____

- _____ : _____

- _____ : _____

- _____ : सेव् (___) _____

- _____ : _____

- _____ : _____

- _____ : _____

5. लट् (Present Tense) in कर्तरि प्रयोगः (Active Voice) with common धातुs

असँ भुवि – अस् to be (2P) in लट् (Present Tense) – कर्तरि-प्रयोगः (Active Voice)

डुकृञ् करणे – कृ to do (8U) in लट् (Present Tense) – कर्तरि-प्रयोगः (Active Voice)

Since कृ is type U, उभयपदी धातुः, two sets of forms are seen; one with परस्मैपद suffixes and the other with आत्मनेपद suffixes.

Topic V – Conjugation in लट् (Present tense)

ज्ञा अवबोधने – ज्ञा to know (9P) in लट् (Present Tense) – कर्तरि-प्रयोगः (Active Voice)

आप्नूँ व्याप्तौ – आप् to pervade (5P) in लट् (Present Tense) – कर्तरि-प्रयोगः (Active Voice)

विदँ ज्ञाने – विद् to know (2P) in लट् (Present Tense) – कर्तरि-प्रयोगः (Active Voice)

There are two forms for each person and number.

43

Topic V – Conjugation in लट् (Present tense)

ब्रूञ् व्यक्तायां वाचि – ब्रू to say (2U) in लट् (Present Tense) – कर्तरि-प्रयोगः (Active Voice)

When the first five परस्मैपद suffixes follow, there are two forms.

डुदाञ् दाने – दा to give (3U) in लट् (Present Tense) – कर्तरि-प्रयोगः (Active Voice)

6. लट् (Present Tense) – कर्मणि प्रयोगः (Passive Voice)

- _____ : दृश ( )
- _____ : _____
- प्रयोगः (voice): कर्तरि-प्रयोगः (passive voice)
- _____ : _____

- _____ : गम् ( )
- _____ : _____
- _____ : _____
- _____ : _____

Topic V – Conjugation in लट् (Present tense)

- _____ : इष् (____) _____
- _____ : _____
- _____ : _____
- _____ : _____

- _____ : ज्ञा (____) _____
- _____ : _____
- _____ : _____
- _____ : _____

Topic VI

Conjugation in other लकारs

1. लिट् (Perfect Past Tense)

भू to be (1P) and अस् to be (2P) in लिट् (Perfect Past Tense) – कर्तरि प्रयोगः (Active Voice)

* अस् becomes "भू" in लिट्.

शुभ् _____

2. लुट् (First Future Tense)

भू to be (1P) and अस् to be (2P) in लुट् (First Future Tense) – कर्तरि प्रयोगः (Active Voice)

* अस् becomes "भू" in लुट्.

पठ् _____

मुद् _____

3. लृट् (Second Future Tense)

भू to be (1P) and अस् to be (2P) in लृट् (First Future Tense) – कर्तरि प्रयोगः (Active Voice)

* अस् becomes "भू" in लृट्.

गम् _____

मुद् _____

4. लोट् (Imperative Mood)

भू सत्तायाम् – भू to be (1P) in लोट् (Imperative Mood) – कर्तरि प्रयोगः (Active Voice)

अस् _____

दृश् _____

स्मृ _____

मुद् _____

गम् _____ – कर्मणि प्रयोगः (Passive Voice)

5. लङ् (Simple Past Tense)

भू सत्तायाम् – भू to be (1P) in लङ् (Simple Past Tense) – कर्तरि प्रयोगः (Active Voice)

अस् _____

गम् _____

वद् _____

जन् _____

गम् _____ – कर्मणि प्रयोगः (Passive Voice)

6. विधिलिङ् (Potential Mood)

भू सत्तायाम् – भू to be (1P) in विधिलिङ् (Potential Mood – कर्तरि प्रयोगः (Active Voice)

अस् _____

गम् _____

वद् _____

वृत् _____

गम् _____ – कर्मणि प्रयोगः (Passive Voice)

7. आशीर्लिङ् (Benedictive Mood)

भू to be (1P) and अस् to be (2P) in आशीर्लिङ् (Benedictive Mood) – कर्तरि प्रयोगः (Active Voice)

* अस् becomes "भू" in आशीर्लिङ्.

8. लुङ् (General Past Tense)

भू to be (1P) and अस् to be (2P) in लुङ् (General Past Tense) – कर्तरि प्रयोगः (Active Voice)

* अस् becomes "भू" in आशीर्लिङ्.

9. लृङ् (Conditional Mood)

भू to be (1P) and अस् to be (2P) in लृङ् (Conditional Mood) – कर्तरि प्रयोगः (Active Voice)

* अस् becomes "भू" in लृङ्.

कृ _____

With परस्मैपद-प्रत्ययs

With आत्मनेपद-प्रत्ययs

Topic VII

The Concept of

Nouns (सुबन्तम् [subantam])

2. Constituents of noun (सुबन्तम् [subantam])

Noun (_____ [_____])

= Nominal base (_____ [_____]) + Nominal suffix (_____ [_____])

3. Classification of प्रातिपदिक [prātipadika]

प्रातिपदिकs are classified in two ways:

i. _____

ii. _____

i. Genders

In Sanskrit language, there are three genders for nouns.

- o Masculine (_____ [_____])

- o Feminine (_____ [_____])

- o Neuter (_____ [_____])

58

4. Nominal suffix (सुप्-प्रत्ययः [sup-pratyayaḥ])

सुप्-प्रत्ययs indicate two things.

<u>i. Case (_____ [_____])</u>

<u>ii. Number (_____ [_____])</u>

There are three numbers (वचनs):

singular (_____ [_____])

dual (_____ [_____])

plural (_____ [_____])

By these two factors (case and number), every suffix of twenty-one सुप्-प्रत्ययs is unique, as seen in the chart below.

Number Case			

सुप्-प्रत्ययs are suffixed to प्रातिपदिक to convey:

i. _____

ii. _____

Topic VIII

Meanings of case endings

(विभक्त्यर्थाः [vibhaktyarthāḥ])

0. Basic concepts of विभक्तिः (Case endings)

☐   7 विभक्तिs are:

विभक्तिः	Case	English term
[ ]		
[ ]		
[ ]		
[ ]		
[ ]		
[ ]		
[ ]		

8. Summary table of विभक्त्यर्थाः

Case / विभक्तिः	Meaning of the case / विभक्त्यर्थाः

Topic IX

Declension of

Vowel-ending Nominal bases

and Pronouns

1. अ-ending in पुंलिङ्ग (masculine) – राम [rāma]

Declension of प्रातिपदिकम् "राम" (Rāma), अकारान्त-पुंलिङ्ग-शब्दः

		1/1	1/2	1/3
		2/1	2/2	2/3
		3/1	3/2	3/3
		4/1	4/2	4/3
		5/1	5/2	5/3
		6/1	6/2	6/3
		7/1	7/2	7/3
		8/1	8/2	8/3

अ-ending masculine (अकारान्त-पुंलिङ्ग-शब्दः – देव (　　　)

————————————————— – पुरुष (　　　)

_____ – लोक (   )

_____ – वेद (   )

2. अ-ending Pronouns in पुंलिङ्ग (masculine) – सर्व [sarva]

प्रातिपदिकम् (nominal base) – सर्व (all) in पुंलिङ्ग (Masculine)

			1/3
	4/1		
	5/1		
			6/3
	7/1		
			8/3

_____ – अन्य (   ) in   (   )

_____ – एक ( ) in ( )

_____ – पर ( ) in ( )

3. Other Pronouns in पुंलिङ्ग (masculine) – तद्, यद्, एतद्, किम्

प्रातिपदिकम् (nominal base) – तद् (that) in पुंलिङ्ग (Masculine)

☐ तद् declines as 'त", अ-ending सर्वनाम, except for 1/1.

	1/1		

The rest declines like सर्व. * There is no vocative.

प्रातिपदिकम् (nominal base) – यद् (that which) in पुंलिङ्ग (Masculine)

☐ यद् declines as 'य", अ-ending सर्वनाम, like सर्व.

It declines like सर्व. * There is no vocative.

प्रातिपदिकम् (nominal base) – एतद् (this) in पुंलिङ्ग (Masculine)

☐ एतद् declines as 'एत', अ-ending सर्वनाम, except for 1/1.

	1/1		

The rest declines like सर्व. * There is no vocative.

प्रातिपदिकम् (nominal base) – किम् (what, interrogative pronoun) in पुंलिङ्ग

☐ किम् declines as 'क', अ-ending सर्वनाम, like सर्व.

It declines like सर्व. * There is no vocative.

☐ When यद् and किम् are used together, it means "whatever".

4. अ-ending in नपुंसकलिङ्ग (neuter) – ज्ञान [jñāna]

प्रातिपदिकम् (nominal base) – ज्ञान (knowledge)

	1/1	1/2	1/3
	2/1	2/2	2/3
	8/1	8/2	8/3

_____ – फल (   )

5. अ-ending Pronouns in नपुंसकलिङ्ग (neuter) – सर्व [sarva]

प्रातिपदिकम् (nominal base) – सर्व (all) in नपुंसकलिङ्ग (Neuter)

	1/1	1/2	1/3
	2/1	2/2	2/3
	8/1	8/2	8/3

_____ – पर (   ) in   (   )

Topic IX – Declension of Vowel-ending Nominal bases and Pronouns

_____ – पूर्व (   ) in   (   )

_____ – अन्य (   ) in   (   )

6. Other Pronouns in नपुंसकलिङ्ग (neuter) – तद्, यद्, एतद्, किम्

प्रातिपदिकम् (nominal base) – तद् (that) in नपुंसकलिङ्ग (Neuter)

- तद् declines as 'त", अ-ending सर्वनाम, except for 1/1 and 2/1.

	1/1		
	2/1		

The rest declines like सर्व. * There is no vocative.

प्रातिपदिकम् (nominal base) – यद् (that which) in नपुंसकलिङ्ग (Neuter)

- यद् declines as 'य", अ-ending सर्वनाम, except for 1/1 and 2/1.

	1/1		
	2/1		

The rest declines like सर्व. * There is no vocative.

प्रातिपदिकम् (nominal base) – एतद् (this) in नपुंसकलिङ्ग (Neuter)

- ☐ एतद् declines as 'एत', अ-ending सर्वनाम, except for 1/1 and 2/1.

	1/1		
	2/1		

The rest declines like सर्व. * There is no vocative.

प्रातिपदिकम् (nominal base) – किम् (what, interrogative pronoun) in नपुंसकलिङ्ग

- ☐ किम् declines as 'क', अ-ending सर्वनाम, except for 1/1 and 2/1.

	1/1		
	2/1		

The rest declines like सर्व. * There is no vocative.

7. इ/उ-ending in पुंलिङ्ग (masculine) – हरि [hari]/गुरु [guru]

प्रातिपदिकम् (nominal base) – हरि (Hari)

_____ – ऋषि (   )

Topic IX – Declension of Vowel-ending Nominal bases and Pronouns

_____ – यति (   )

_____ – गिरि (   )

प्रातिपदिकम् (nominal base) – गुरु (teacher)

_____ – मुमुक्षु (   )

Topic IX – Declension of Vowel-ending Nominal bases and Pronouns

_____ – हेतु (   )

_____ – धातु (   )

Modifications of इ/उ of इ/उ-ending प्रातिपदिकs

विभक्तिः \ वचनम्	एकवचनम्	द्विवचनम्	बहुवचनम्
प्रथमा (1st case)			
द्वितीया (2nd case)			
तृतीया (3rd case)			
चतुर्थी (4th case)			
पञ्चमी (5th case)			
षष्ठी (6th case)			
सप्तमी (7th case)			
सम्बोधनम् (Vocative)			

8. ऋ-ending in पुंलिङ्ग (masculine) – कर्तृ [kartṛ]

प्रातिपदिकम् (nominal base) – कर्तृ (doer)

_____ – ज्ञातृ (   )

_____ – प्रमातृ (   )

_____ – हन्तृ (   )

सुप्-प्रत्ययs (nominal suffixes) without इत् (indicatory) letters

	Singular	Dual	Plural
1st case			
2nd case			
3rd case			
4th case			
5th case			
6th case			
7th case			

Three sections in masculine and feminine

	Singular	Dual	Plural
1st case	स् [s]	औ [au]	अस् [as]
2nd case	अम् [am]	औ [au]	
3rd case			
4th case			
5th case			
6th case			
7th case			

The प्रत्यय in this section of the chart is termed _____ [_____].

The अङ्ग in this section of the chart is termed _____ [_____].

The अङ्ग in this section of the chart is termed _____ [_____].

9. आ-ending in स्त्रीलिङ्ग (feminine) – गङ्गा [gaṅgā]

प्रातिपदिकम् (nominal base) – गङ्गा (gaṅgā)

_____ – गुहा (   )

_____ – अवस्था (   )

_____ – क्रिया (   )

10. आ-ending Pronouns in स्त्रीलिङ्ग (feminine) – सर्वा [sarvā]

प्रातिपदिकम् (nominal base) – सर्वा (all)

	4/1		
	5/1		
	6/1		6/3
	7/1		

_____ – अन्या (   )

11. Other Pronouns in स्त्रीलिङ्ग (feminine) – तद्, यद्, एतद्, किम्

प्रातिपदिकम् (nominal base) – तद् (that)

☐ तद् declines as 'ता', आ-ending सर्वनाम, except for 1/1.

	1/1		

The rest declines like सर्वा. * There is no vocative.

प्रातिपदिकम् (nominal base) – यद् (that which)

☐ यद् declines as 'या', आ-ending सर्वनाम, like सर्वा.

It declines like सर्वा. * There is no vocative.

प्रातिपदिकम् (nominal base) – एतद् (this)

☐ एतद् declines as 'एता", आ-ending सर्वनाम, except for 1/1.

	1/1		

The rest declines like सर्वा. * There is no vocative.

प्रातिपदिकम् (nominal base) – किम् (what, interrogative pronoun)

☐ किम् declines as 'का", आ-ending सर्वनाम, like सर्वा.

It declines like सर्वा. * There is no vocative.

12. ई-ending in स्त्रीलिङ्ग (feminine) – नदी [nadī]

प्रातिपदिकम् (nominal base) – नदी (river)

_____ – पृथवी (   )

_____ – कर्त्री (   )

_____ – सती (   )

13. इ-ending in स्त्रीलिङ्ग (feminine) – मति [mati]

प्रातिपदिकम् (nominal base) – मति (intellect)

			2/3
	3/1		
	4/1		
	5/1		
	6/1		
	7/1		

The rest declines like हरि in पुंलिङ्ग.

_____ – दृष्टि (   )

89

_____ – बुद्धि (   )

_____ – श्रुति (   )

14. Pronoun – इदम् [idam]

प्रातिपदिकम् (nominal base) – इदम् (this) - पुंलिङ्गे (in masculine)

☐ इदम् declines as 'अ", except as indicated below in black.

		1/1	1/2	1/3
		2/1	2/2	2/3
		3/1		3/3
			6/2	
			7/2	

The rest declines like सर्व. * There is no vocative.

प्रातिपदिकम् (nominal base) – इदम् (this) - नपुंसके (in neuter)

		1/1	1/2	1/3
		2/1	2/2	2/3

The rest declines like इदम् in पुंलिङ्ग. * There is no vocative.

प्रातिपदिकम् (nominal base) – इदम् (this) - स्त्रीलिङ्गे (in feminine)

☐ इदम् declines as 'आ", except as indicated below in black.

		1/1		1/2		1/3
		2/1		2/2		2/3
		3/1				
				6/2		
				7/2		

The rest declines like सर्वा.

15. Pronoun – अदस् [adas]

प्रातिपदिकम् (nominal base) – अदस् (that) - पुंलिङ्गे (in masculine)

	1/1	1/2	1/3
	2/1	2/2	2/3
	3/1	3/2	3/3
	4/1	4/2	4/3
	5/1	5/2	5/3
	6/1	6/2	6/3
	7/1	7/2	7/3

प्रातिपदिकम् (nominal base) – अदस् (that) - नपुंसके (in neuter)

	1/1	1/2	1/3
	2/1	2/2	2/3

The rest declines like अदस् in पुंलिङ्ग. * There is no vocative.

93

प्रातिपदिकम् (nominal base) – अदस् (that) - स्त्रीलिङ्गे (in feminine)

	1/1	1/2	1/3
	2/1	2/2	2/3
	3/1	3/2	3/3
	4/1	4/2	4/3
	5/1	5/2	5/3
	6/1	6/2	6/3
	7/1	7/2	7/3

16. Pronouns – युष्मद् [yuṣmad], अस्मद् [asmad]

☐ युष्मद् (you) and अस्मद् (I, we) have the same forms in all 3 लिङ्गs (genders).

प्रातिपदिकम् (nominal base) – युष्मद् (you)

		1/1		1/2		1/3
		2/1		2/2		2/3
		3/1		3/2		3/3
		4/1		4/2		4/3
		5/1		5/2		5/3
		6/1		6/2		6/3
		7/1		7/2		7/3

प्रातिपदिकम् (nominal base) – अस्मद् (I, we)

		1/1		1/2		1/3
		2/1		2/2		2/3
		3/1		3/2		3/3
		4/1		4/2		4/3
		5/1		5/2		5/3
		6/1		6/2		6/3
		7/1		7/2		7/3

* There is no vocative.

<u>अन्वादेशः (referring again) of "इदम्" (this) and "एतद्" (this) in masculine</u>

	एकवचनम्	द्विवचनम्	बहुवचनम्
प्रथमा (1st case)			
द्वितीया (2nd case)	2/1	2/2	2/3
तृतीया (3rd case)	3/1		
चतुर्थी (4th case)			
पञ्चमी (5th case)			
षष्ठी (6th case)		6/2	
सप्तमी (7th case)		7/2	

The rest declines as usual.

<u>अन्वादेशः (referring again) of "इदम्" (this) and "एतद्" (this) in neuter</u>

	एकवचनम्	द्विवचनम्	बहुवचनम्
प्रथमा (1st case)			
द्वितीया (2nd case)	2/1	2/2	2/3

The rest (excepting 1st case) declines like masculine.

<u>अन्वादेशः (referring again) of "इदम्" (this) and "एतद्" (this) in feminine</u>

	एकवचनम्	द्विवचनम्	बहुवचनम्
प्रथमा (1st case)			
द्वितीया (2nd case)	2/1	2/2	2/3
तृतीया (3rd case)	3/1		
चतुर्थी (4th case)			
पञ्चमी (5th case)			
षष्ठी (6th case)		6/2	
सप्तमी (7th case)		7/2	

The rest declines as usual.

Topic X

Declension of

Consonant-ending Nominal bases

सुप्-प्रत्ययs (nominal suffixes) without इत् (indicatory) letters

	Singular	Dual	Plural
1st case			
2nd case			
3rd case			
4th case			
5th case			
6th case			
7th case			

सुप्-प्रत्ययs (nominal suffixes) modified for declension in neuter

	Singular	Dual	Plural
1st case			
2nd case			

Topic X – Declension of Consonant-ending Nominal bases

Three sections in masculine and feminine

विभक्तिः \ वचनम्	एकवचनम् (Singular)	द्विवचनम् (Dual)	बहुवचनम् (Plural)
प्रथमा (1st case)	स् [s]	औ [au]	अस् [as]
द्वितीया (2nd case)	अम् [am]	औ [au]	
तृतीया (3rd case)			
चतुर्थी (4th case)			
पञ्चमी (5th case)			
षष्ठी (6th case)			
सप्तमी (7th case)			

Three sections in neuter

विभक्तिः \ वचनम्	एकवचनम् (Singular)	द्विवचनम् (Dual)	बहुवचनम् (Plural)
प्रथमा (1st case)			इ [i]
द्वितीया (2nd case)			इ [i]

The rest is the same as masculine and feminine.

The प्रत्यय in this section of the chart is termed _____ [_____].

The अङ्ग in this section of the chart is termed _____ [_____].

The अङ्ग in this section of the chart is termed _____ [_____].

1. ण्-ending in पुंलिङ्ग (masculine)/स्त्रीलिङ्ग (feminine) – सुगण् [sugaṇ]

प्रातिपदिकम् (nominal base) – सुगण् (counting well)

	1/1	1/2	1/3
	2/1	2/2	2/3
	3/1	3/2	3/3
	4/1	4/2	4/3
	5/1	5/2	5/3
	6/1	6/2	6/3
	7/1	7/2	7/3
	8/1	8/2	8/3

_____ – यण् (   )

	1/1	1/2	1/3
	2/1	2/2	2/3
	3/1	3/2	3/3
	4/1	4/2	4/3
	5/1	5/2	5/3
	6/1	6/2	6/3
	7/1	7/2	7/3
	8/1	8/2	8/3

Topic X – Declension of Consonant-ending Nominal bases

_____ – हल् (   )

		1/1		1/2		1/3
		2/1		2/2		2/3
		3/1		3/2		3/3
		4/1		4/2		4/3
		5/1		5/2		5/3
		6/1		6/2		6/3
		7/1		7/2		7/3
		8/1		8/2		8/3

_____ – एङ् (   )

		1/1		1/2		1/3
		2/1		2/2		2/3
		3/1		3/2		3/3
		4/1		4/2		4/3
		5/1		5/2		5/3
		6/1		6/2		6/3
		7/1		7/2		7/3
		8/1		8/2		8/3

2. त्/द्/ध्/भ्-ending in पुंलिङ्ग (masculine)/स्त्रीलिङ्ग (feminine) – मरुत् [marut]

प्रातिपदिकम् (nominal base) – मरुत् (the wind god)

		1/1	1/2		1/3
		2/1	2/2		2/3
		3/1	3/2		3/3
		4/1	4/2		4/3
		5/1	5/2		5/3
		6/1	6/2		6/3
		7/1	7/2		7/3
		8/1	8/2		8/3

_____ – अत् ( )

		1/1	1/2		1/3
		2/1	2/2		2/3
		3/1	3/2		3/3
		4/1	4/2		4/3
		5/1	5/2		5/3
		6/1	6/2		6/3
		7/1	7/2		7/3
		8/1	8/2		8/3

Topic X – Declension of Consonant-ending Nominal bases

_____ – विद्युत् (   )

		1/1		1/2		1/3
		2/1		2/2		2/3
		3/1		3/2		3/3
		4/1		4/2		4/3
		5/1		5/2		5/3
		6/1		6/2		6/3
		7/1		7/2		7/3
		8/1		8/2		8/3

_____ – मृद् (   )

		1/1		1/2		1/3
		2/1		2/2		2/3
		3/1		3/2		3/3
		4/1		4/2		4/3
		5/1		5/2		5/3
		6/1		6/2		6/3
		7/1		7/2		7/3
		8/1		8/2		8/3

_____ – सर्वविद् (   )

		1/1		1/2		1/3
		2/1		2/2		2/3
		3/1		3/2		3/3
		4/1		4/2		4/3
		5/1		5/2		5/3
		6/1		6/2		6/3
		7/1		7/2		7/3
		8/1		8/2		8/3

_____ – उपनिषद् (   )

		1/1		1/2		1/3
		2/1		2/2		2/3
		3/1		3/2		3/3
		4/1		4/2		4/3
		5/1		5/2		5/3
		6/1		6/2		6/3
		7/1		7/2		7/3
		8/1		8/2		8/3

_____ – समिध् (   )

		1/1	1/2	1/3
		2/1	2/2	2/3
		3/1	3/2	3/3
		4/1	4/2	4/3
		5/1	5/2	5/3
		6/1	6/2	6/3
		7/1	7/2	7/3
		8/1	8/2	8/3

_____ –अनुष्टुभ् (   )

		1/1	1/2	1/3
		2/1	2/2	2/3
		3/1	3/2	3/3
		4/1	4/2	4/3
		5/1	5/2	5/3
		6/1	6/2	6/3
		7/1	7/2	7/3
		8/1	8/2	8/3

3. च/ज्-ending in पुंलिङ्ग (masculine)/स्त्रीलिङ्ग (feminine) – ऋच् [ṛc]

प्रातिपदिकम् (nominal base) – ऋच् (hymn, mantra)

		1/1	1/2	1/3
		2/1	2/2	2/3
		3/1	3/2	3/3
		4/1	4/2	4/3
		5/1	5/2	5/3
		6/1	6/2	6/3
		7/1	7/2	7/3
		8/1	8/2	8/3

_____ –वाच् (   )

		1/1	1/2	1/3
		2/1	2/2	2/3
		3/1	3/2	3/3
		4/1	4/2	4/3
		5/1	5/2	5/3
		6/1	6/2	6/3
		7/1	7/2	7/3
		8/1	8/2	8/3

_____ –ऋत्विज् (   )

		1/1	1/2	1/3
		2/1	2/2	2/3
		3/1	3/2	3/3
		4/1	4/2	4/3
		5/1	5/2	5/3
		6/1	6/2	6/3
		7/1	7/2	7/3
		8/1	8/2	8/3

_____ –भिषज् (   )

		1/1	1/2	1/3
		2/1	2/2	2/3
		3/1	3/2	3/3
		4/1	4/2	4/3
		5/1	5/2	5/3
		6/1	6/2	6/3
		7/1	7/2	7/3
		8/1	8/2	8/3

4. इन्-ending in पुंल्लिङ्ग/स्त्रीलिङ्ग – योगिन् [yogin]/योगिनी [yoginī]

प्रातिपदिकम् (nominal base) – योगिन् (one who has योग)

		1/1		1/2		1/3
		2/1		2/2		2/3
		3/1		3/2		3/3
		4/1		4/2		4/3
		5/1		5/2		5/3
		6/1		6/2		6/3
		7/1		7/2		7/3
		8/1		8/2		8/3

_____ –अधकारिन् (   )

		1/1		1/2		1/3
		2/1		2/2		2/3
		3/1		3/2		3/3
		4/1		4/2		4/3
		5/1		5/2		5/3
		6/1		6/2		6/3
		7/1		7/2		7/3
		8/1		8/2		8/3

_____ –ज्ञानिन् (   )

		1/1	1/2	1/3
		2/1	2/2	2/3
		3/1	3/2	3/3
		4/1	4/2	4/3
		5/1	5/2	5/3
		6/1	6/2	6/3
		7/1	7/2	7/3
		8/1	8/2	8/3

_____ –प्राणिन् (   )

		1/1	1/2	1/3
		2/1	2/2	2/3
		3/1	3/2	3/3
		4/1	4/2	4/3
		5/1	5/2	5/3
		6/1	6/2	6/3
		7/1	7/2	7/3
		8/1	8/2	8/3

5. मत्/वत्-ending in पुंलिङ्ग/स्त्रीलिङ्ग – भगवत् [bhagavat]/भगवती [bhagavatī]

प्रातिपदिकम् (nominal base) – भगवत् (one who has भग)

	1/1	1/2	1/3
	2/1	2/2	2/3
	3/1	3/2	3/3
	4/1	4/2	4/3
	5/1	5/2	5/3
	6/1	6/2	6/3
	7/1	7/2	7/3
	8/1	8/2	8/3

_____ –धनवत् (   )

	1/1	1/2	1/3
	2/1	2/2	2/3
	3/1	3/2	3/3
	4/1	4/2	4/3
	5/1	5/2	5/3
	6/1	6/2	6/3
	7/1	7/2	7/3
	8/1	8/2	8/3

_____ –भवत् (   )

	1/1	1/2	1/3
	2/1	2/2	2/3
	3/1	3/2	3/3
	4/1	4/2	4/3
	5/1	5/2	5/3
	6/1	6/2	6/3
	7/1	7/2	7/3
	8/1	8/2	8/3

_____ –बुद्धिमत् (   )

	1/1	1/2	1/3
	2/1	2/2	2/3
	3/1	3/2	3/3
	4/1	4/2	4/3
	5/1	5/2	5/3
	6/1	6/2	6/3
	7/1	7/2	7/3
	8/1	8/2	8/3

6. शतृँ-ending in पुंलिङ्ग/स्त्रीलिङ्ग – सत् [sat]/सती [satī]

प्रातिपदिकम् (nominal base) – सत् (being)

	1/1	1/2	1/3
	2/1	2/2	2/3
	3/1	3/2	3/3
	4/1	4/2	4/3
	5/1	5/2	5/3
	6/1	6/2	6/3
	7/1	7/2	7/3
	8/1	8/2	8/3

_____ –पचत् (   )

	1/1	1/2	1/3
	2/1	2/2	2/3
	3/1	3/2	3/3
	4/1	4/2	4/3
	5/1	5/2	5/3
	6/1	6/2	6/3
	7/1	7/2	7/3
	8/1	8/2	8/3

111

Topic X – Declension of Consonant-ending Nominal bases

_____ –पश्यत् (   )

		1/1		1/2		1/3
		2/1		2/2		2/3
		3/1		3/2		3/3
		4/1		4/2		4/3
		5/1		5/2		5/3
		6/1		6/2		6/3
		7/1		7/2		7/3
		8/1		8/2		8/3

_____ –ध्यायत् (   )

		1/1		1/2		1/3
		2/1		2/2		2/3
		3/1		3/2		3/3
		4/1		4/2		4/3
		5/1		5/2		5/3
		6/1		6/2		6/3
		7/1		7/2		7/3
		8/1		8/2		8/3

7. अन्-ending in पुंलिङ्ग (masculine) – आत्मन् [ātman]

प्रातिपदिकम् (nominal base) – आत्मन् (oneself)

	1/1	1/2	1/3
	2/1	2/2	2/3
	3/1	3/2	3/3
	4/1	4/2	4/3
	5/1	5/2	5/3
	6/1	6/2	6/3
	7/1	7/2	7/3
	8/1	8/2	8/3

_____ –ब्रह्मन् (   )

	1/1	1/2	1/3
	2/1	2/2	2/3
	3/1	3/2	3/3
	4/1	4/2	4/3
	5/1	5/2	5/3
	6/1	6/2	6/3
	7/1	7/2	7/3
	8/1	8/2	8/3

_____ –राजन् (   )

	1/1	1/2	1/3
	2/1	2/2	2/3
	3/1	3/2	3/3
	4/1	4/2	4/3
	5/1	5/2	5/3
	6/1	6/2	6/3
	7/1	7/2	7/3
	8/1	8/2	8/3

_____ –महमन् (   )

	1/1	1/2	1/3
	2/1	2/2	2/3
	3/1	3/2	3/3
	4/1	4/2	4/3
	5/1	5/2	5/3
	6/1	6/2	6/3
	7/1	7/2	7/3
	8/1	8/2	8/3

8. अन्-ending in नपुंसकलिङ्ग (neuter) – ब्रह्मन् [brahman]

प्रातिपदिकम् (nominal base) – ब्रह्मन् (brahman)

		1/1		1/2		1/3
		2/1		2/2		2/3
		3/1		3/2		3/3
		4/1		4/2		4/3
		5/1		5/2		5/3
		6/1		6/2		6/3
		7/1		7/2		7/3
		8/1		8/2		8/3

_____ –कर्मन् (   )

		1/1		1/2		1/3
		2/1		2/2		2/3
		3/1		3/2		3/3
		4/1		4/2		4/3
		5/1		5/2		5/3
		6/1		6/2		6/3
		7/1		7/2		7/3
		8/1		8/2		8/3

115

_____ –जन्मन् (   )

		1/1	1/2	1/3
		2/1	2/2	2/3
		3/1	3/2	3/3
		4/1	4/2	4/3
		5/1	5/2	5/3
		6/1	6/2	6/3
		7/1	7/2	7/3
		8/1	8/2	8/3

_____ –नामन् (   )

		1/1	1/2	1/3
		2/1	2/2	2/3
		3/1	3/2	3/3
		4/1	4/2	4/3
		5/1	5/2	5/3
		6/1	6/2	6/3
		7/1	7/2	7/3
		8/1	8/2	8/3

9. अस्-ending in नपुंसकलिङ्ग (neuter) – मनस् [manas]

प्रातिपदिकम् (nominal base) – मनस् (mind)

		1/1		1/2		1/3
		2/1		2/2		2/3
		3/1		3/2		3/3
		4/1		4/2		4/3
		5/1		5/2		5/3
		6/1		6/2		6/3
		7/1		7/2		7/3
		8/1		8/2		8/3

_____ – तेजस् (   )

		1/1		1/2		1/3
		2/1		2/2		2/3
		3/1		3/2		3/3
		4/1		4/2		4/3
		5/1		5/2		5/3
		6/1		6/2		6/3
		7/1		7/2		7/3
		8/1		8/2		8/3

Topic X – Declension of Consonant-ending Nominal bases

_____ – तमस् (   )

		1/1		1/2		1/3
		2/1		2/2		2/3
		3/1		3/2		3/3
		4/1		4/2		4/3
		5/1		5/2		5/3
		6/1		6/2		6/3
		7/1		7/2		7/3
		8/1		8/2		8/3

_____ – श्रेयस् (   )

		1/1		1/2		1/3
		2/1		2/2		2/3
		3/1		3/2		3/3
		4/1		4/2		4/3
		5/1		5/2		5/3
		6/1		6/2		6/3
		7/1		7/2		7/3
		8/1		8/2		8/3

10. इष्/उष्-ending in नपुंसकलिङ्ग (neuter) – ज्योतिस् [jyotis]/चक्षुस् [caksus]

प्रातिपदिकम् (nominal base) – ज्योतिष् (light)

		1/1		1/2		1/3
		2/1		2/2		2/3
		3/1		3/2		3/3
		4/1		4/2		4/3
		5/1		5/2		5/3
		6/1		6/2		6/3
		7/1		7/2		7/3
		8/1		8/2		8/3

_____ – हविष् (   )

		1/1		1/2		1/3
		2/1		2/2		2/3
		3/1		3/2		3/3
		4/1		4/2		4/3
		5/1		5/2		5/3
		6/1		6/2		6/3
		7/1		7/2		7/3
		8/1		8/2		8/3

Topic X – Declension of Consonant-ending Nominal bases

_____ – चक्षुष् (   )

		1/1		1/2		1/3
		2/1		2/2		2/3
		3/1		3/2		3/3
		4/1		4/2		4/3
		5/1		5/2		5/3
		6/1		6/2		6/3
		7/1		7/2		7/3
		8/1		8/2		8/3

_____ – यजुष् (   )

		1/1		1/2		1/3
		2/1		2/2		2/3
		3/1		3/2		3/3
		4/1		4/2		4/3
		5/1		5/2		5/3
		6/1		6/2		6/3
		7/1		7/2		7/3
		8/1		8/2		8/3

11. अस्-ending in पुंलिङ्ग (masculine) – चन्द्रमस् [candramas]

प्रातिपदिकम् (nominal base) – चन्द्रमस् (moon)

		1/1		1/2		1/3
		2/1		2/2		2/3
		3/1		3/2		3/3
		4/1		4/2		4/3
		5/1		5/2		5/3
		6/1		6/2		6/3
		7/1		7/2		7/3
		8/1		8/2		8/3

_____ – वेधस् (   )

		1/1		1/2		1/3
		2/1		2/2		2/3
		3/1		3/2		3/3
		4/1		4/2		4/3
		5/1		5/2		5/3
		6/1		6/2		6/3
		7/1		7/2		7/3
		8/1		8/2		8/3

Exercise

_____ – सुमनस् (   )

		1/1	1/2	1/3
		2/1	2/2	2/3
		3/1	3/2	3/3
		4/1	4/2	4/3
		5/1	5/2	5/3
		6/1	6/2	6/3
		7/1	7/2	7/3
		8/1	8/2	8/3

_____ – नचिकेतस् (   )

		1/1	1/2	1/3
		2/1	2/2	2/3
		3/1	3/2	3/3
		4/1	4/2	4/3
		5/1	5/2	5/3
		6/1	6/2	6/3
		7/1	7/2	7/3
		8/1	8/2	8/3

Printed in Poland
by Amazon Fulfillment
Poland Sp. z o.o., Wrocław